William Darwin Crabb

Lyrics of the Golden West

William Darwin Crabb

Lyrics of the Golden West

ISBN/EAN: 9783744795920

Printed in Europe, USA, Canada, Australia, Japan

Cover: Foto ©Thomas Meinert / pixelio.de

More available books at **www.hansebooks.com**

LYRICS

OF THE

GOLDEN WEST.

BY

W? D? CRABB.

SAN FRANCISCO:
THE WHITAKER & RAY COMPANY,
(INCORPORATED.)
1898.

CONTENTS.

	PAGE.
DEDICATION—ESTHER, THE IDEAL	7
CALIFORNIA SUNRISE	13
CAPE HORN OF THE SIERRAS	14
ROCKS OF MONTEREY (From the Overland Monthly)	15
DRIVEN FROM EDEN—TALE OF A PIONEER	17
IN LOS ANGELES—TO ESTHER	27
LAURA OF PARADISE	31
THE VALLEY OF PEACE	33
TWO DEPARTURES—TAMALPAIS	36
CITY OF THE GOLDEN GATE	37
SHASTA	39
SACRAMENTO VALLEY IN SPRING	41
IN THE DESERT—OVERLAND	42
HUMBOLDT LAKE	44
THE RANCHER'S STORY	45
THE ISHMAELITE	48
EDGAR A. POE	58
A DIRGE	60
NOLETHA	62
THAT DREAMLESS SLEEP	65

CONTENTS.

	PAGE.
A Double Prophecy	75
Esther	81
To Esther (From Locke's National Monthly)	83
My Far-Away	85
Confidence	87
Thine Eyes	90
My Flowers	93
Annette	96
Since Thou Art Not Here	98
I May Not Stay	100
Agnes	101
My Young Wild Rhyme	103
By-and-By	104
A Star of Reminder	104
Fact vs. Fiction	106
Live and Let Live	112
The White Crane	114
Death of the Old Professor	116
Telouchkine	118
Wayside Flowers	120

LYRICS

OF THE

GOLDEN WEST.

ESTHER, THE IDEAL.

DEDICATORY.

To Her
  who first a song, a voice,
 Accordant with seraphic lyre
From Heaven came to win her choice,
 And sing her being thro' my heart,
  And make anew my soul acute,
 Enkindling with angelic fire—
  Voice sweeter than the mellow lute—
Song artless, yet the perfect art;
To her these songs I set apart.

To Her
  whose eyes came beaming light
 And love and dawning's quick surprise
Into my love-dead soul of night—
Eyes rich with all hues mingling clear;
  Benignant eyes, dear blue-and-brown;
 Keats-emerald eyes; sweet violet eyes;
  Eyes speaking from the soul deep down;
Those wonder-eyes, kind lamps of cheer—
To her these songs I offer here!

To Her
of rich carnelian lips,
Kiss pure as warm carnation's kiss
On honey-dews the sunrise sips—
And face whose smile of ruby light
To many weary sunless hearts
Brings hope-inspiring tropic bliss
And every laughing joy imparts
And dapples leaves and flowers with bright—
To her these rhythmic lines I write.

To Her
of fonder queenlier charm
Than Esther's charms, humanely royal,
A crownless regal Grace in form,
Yet diademed with priceless crown,
Rare gems upon her queenly crest
Of mind and heart, divinely loyal;
A placid harbor is her breast,
A great good heart ne'er anger-blown
My anchored heart may trust the best—
Round her these sprays of song are strown,
To her this wreath of love is thrown.

To Her
of Grecian form and face,
The sculptor's dreamed ideal glory,
With Venus' limbs and Helen's grace,
Unstained as vestal maids of Rome,
Revealing all the charms of now

And all the dreams of classic story—
   Who lifts her hands in blessings' vow
Above my spirit's temple-dome;
I bring this blushing book of bloom
To her, my heart's one only home!

To Her
      of iridescent bright
  Serene celestial gifts of mind,
To her, the spirit exquisite,
To her the measureless in loves
    That move my being with their thrill—
  Who seeth all, yet seemeth blind
  When seeming blind is mercy-kind!
    Imperial force of heart and will,
Yet gentler than the pretty dove's
Meek notes of pathos thro' the groves—
To her with songs he comes who roves!

To Her
      (tho' years I roam afar
  Unrestful as in primal age
The ark-sent dove 'neath sun and star
Roves o'er the waste that all engirds),
    My heart is held, tho' unconfined—
  To her, the wiser than the sage,
    I bring these poems love-enshrined,
    One book her blessing hath entwined,
Fond notes as songs of dying birds
At sunset—plaintive timid words!

Yet Her
   bright name might make them great;
For living in her thoughts and words
And name is moving thro' the gate
Of rooms resplendent with all bliss,
  Grand furnishings of regal mind;
And, as her halo there engirds
  The singer, songs must be refined—
Transfigured by *this* Esther's kiss
They must be budding great by *this*.
To her, my Love the first the last,
These artless rhymes I meekly cast!

LYRICS

OF THE

GOLDEN WEST.

CALIFORNIA SUNRISE.

A California sunrise, over-fair!
   See, scarlet-colored margins fringed with
       green!
Lo! fields of red and crimson bordered there!
   Here, blue expanses spanned with whitened
       sheen!
Lo! yellow banners floating in the air!
   Now, purple pastures sweet as eye hath
       seen!
Here, pink as blossoms mellow with delight!
O many-hued, sky-ocean's painted Bight,
Bent like Benin against the shore of night!

CAPE HORN OF THE SIERRAS.

Swift as a hawk we sweep around
Where God's battlements descend,
Till cliffs rest on blooming ground
In the growing vale below;
Till this Eden to the eyes
Seems as distant as the skies;
Towering summits seem to blend
With the stars that circle low,—
Blend, and motionless attend.

Circling round so high and swift,
On this mid-suspended rim,
E'en the vale below lies dim,
And the living seem to shift
In mid-shadow, while we drift
Near where planets smile above;
And the heart with tender love
In its fancy would address them,
In its rapturous joy caress them,—
And the heart, its love confessing,
Would on Nature's heart, caressing,
Lay its silent hands in blessing.
But the soul feels the Divine,
Begs forgiveness by a sign,
Bows in awe at Nature's shrine.

ROCKS OF MONTEREY.

Brown rocks, frayed edges of the lands,
    Enfigured with a netted work
    Of woods of pine, where blossoms lurk
Beneath fern leaves as 'neath green hands,—

Worn rocks, the finger-raveled edges
    By finger-tips of Monterey,
    A queenly hand, the mobile bay,
More gemmed than princess's hand with pledges,—

Lorn rocks, so torn and fringed by fingers,—
    In-carved with shapes and shadings rare,
    Arranged in color-patterns fair,—
One turns to go, yet ever lingers!—

Gray rocks, upon whose foldings grand
    Made ivory-smooth by sweeping spray,
    The fingers of the tidal bay
Play organ-tunes along the strand,—

Rough rocks, yet in perspective seen,
    A girth of every gorgeous hue
    And mellow shades wrought thro' and thro'
Of purple-blue and water-green,—

Lone rocks, the chosen, safe retreat
    For shy unbosomings of love,

While stars, and white, thin mists above
Give beauty to the water's fleet,

And, woman-wise and man-discreet,
    The sympathetic, bounding seas
    On rocks, stern-kind in sympathies,
More loud than lovers' voices beat.

How o'er the granite keys they play!
    These rhythmic fingers pearly white,
    With rings of emerald and light,
Topaz and amethystine ray.

Thou beauteous hand, thou matchless bay,
I love thy jeweled glow, thy spray,
Thy myriad splendors in the day,
Thy bridal omens, when the drifted
Star-gems so fairy-like are sifted.

I sit the fringèd rocks among;
I feel thy finger-touch magnetic;
I see thee weaving things prophetic,—
All thoughts profound, sublime, pathetic,
Strength for the old, joy for the young!
  .

DRIVEN FROM EDEN.

TALE OF A PIONEER.

Ah! Time is a heartless intruder
That ruthlessly trudges behind one,
And tramples and crushes to splinters
The painted glass-figures of fancy—
The castles in Spain of the dreamer,
In youth and the budding of manhood:
So how can I gather a story
To-day out of glittering fragments,
Once perfect and brilliant of color
In youth, when the earlier fancies
Lay fairer than roses around me?
Now dim are the dreams of my childhood,
And faded the follies of love-days.

I.

Far back lie the realms of my childhood,
Divine with the promise of love-days,
In the meadows that one of the poets
Pronounced, in his ecstasy, Eden—
Where tides of the beautiful grasses
Of prairies, with glorified blossoms,
Shook hands with the tides of the waters,

And kissed to the kiss of Vermilion—
There prairies are dotted with timber,
As islands deep-green in the ocean:
'Twas there in the breeze and the shadow
Of one of those islands of forest
She dwelt, who was queen of all beauty,
Eulalie, the pride of Vermilion.

Birds floated around and above her
And swung on their pinions of purple,
And all the rich hues under heaven;
They chirped on the branches a message
Of "peace to Eulalie!" and freighted
The air with their languorous love-lays.
The meadow-larks swayed, at a distance,
On stems of the riotous dock-weeds.
'Twas *peace* in the sound of the breezes,
And *peace* in the caroling voices
Of birds in the peace of the tree-tops.
'Twas peace in the whispering grasses;
And delicate voices of waters
Sang *peace*, to the lulling of lilies
Whose peace was the charm of their petals.
'Twas peace unexplored in the star-lands;
With only a breach of their promise
Of peace, as was seen in the falling
Of a meteor at eve, as if sorrow
Had crept into loves of the planets,
And so, now and then in the twilight
A star fell from out of the cluster

Down to night of eternal despairing!—
'Twas peace in the voices of Nature.
'Twas peace in the night and the morning,
And peace all the day and the even.
And peace is the essence of beauty.
Peace, white-armed, sweet peace is the goddess
That soars o'er the passions that rend us—
That deadens the spirit of hatred—
Of jealously, envy, ambition!
Yea, peace, that maketh contentment!
Such peace was in soul of Eulalie,
Whose prayer was, "*May God's peace be with you!*"

I dwelt on the river Vermilion,
Not far from the home of Eulalie—
O why should my spirit awaken,
To follow the feet of an angel?
Then toss on its pillow of passion?
My love was as pure as the heavens,
And true as its blueness of beauty.
But I was devoid of the graces
And ways that should win her affection.
My gait was uncouth; and uncomely
My form; and the money to cover,
My many defects still was lacking.
What charm hid in dusky complexion?
Or coarse hair, as straight as the rushes?
Then why should my spirit awaken

To toss on its pillow of passion?
Ah! was it, as coldly was told me
By one who had power to do evil,
Because (it was false as the wine-cup)!
I saw through the eyes of a dreamer!

But she, she was sweet as the blossoms,
As pure as the buds of the lilies
Caressing the flow of Vermilion.
The smiling, that chased back her laughter,
Rippled like the brook; and it tinted
Her features, expressive, as twilight
Doth chase down the sunset and tinteth
The skies from which Helios retreated!

Alas! now to find that my fancy
Is not as it was; and that somehow,
My power of impassioned expression
Is not as it was in those love-days!
Alas! that the eyes of Eulalie,—
Yea, *all* her enrapturing beauties
Have faded so far into distance;
They are dim through the mists of the mountains
Of pleasure—are dim and uncertain
Thro' smoke of the desolate valleys
Of humiliation and sorrows!
My words are grown heavy as iron
Muse! give me the words that are lacking
To tell what I saw in Eulalie,

So glorified fair with the touches
Of love from the heart of—a dreamer?
But, to-day the dear view is uncertain,
Her form interchanges with others,
Who thrust their dim faces between us,
And smile as they claim recognition!
Yes, to-day, her dear voice is uncertain,
And comes like an echo of echo!
It paineth me sore to distinguish
Her voice from the voices of many
That come from their shadow of waiting,
And call, through an ocean of distance,
And claim—do they get it?—remembrance.

Tell me why war these opposite forces,
Opposing all goodness by evil—
Opposing the sweet by the bitter?

How young, yet how ardent are lovers!
Love wakens the chords in some spirits,
That quiver, with flashes resplendent,
And sound in a lyric of beauty,
Till ending in music of heaven;
In some, tune is wakened in sweetness,
To die in harsh iteration
Of tunes that are dirges to pleasure!—

* * * * *

Come closer; my voice, it grows weaker—
Come closer, and listen; for somehow,

Now faces and voices that mingled
And made my remembrance uncertain
Are clear for the moment to mem'ry—
And, somehow, the mists of these mountains
Of pleasure, the smoke in the valleys
Of humiliation and sorrows
Are breaking away, and my fancies
Shine clear on the banks of Vermilion!
I see now the first of life plainly;
'Tis strange that the commonest trifle,
Sometimes, is remembered for ages,
While deeds we call great are forgotten!—
I went to the home of Eulalie;
I went in my youth burning blushes—
And, Oh! with a sort of foreboding!
We met; and I knew, by the clinging
Of lips and their passionate pulses,
And more by the wonderful kindness
That shone in her eyes, who was victor.

We wooed on the banks of Vermilion.
We called to the fish in the river
Alluring them up to the margin.
The birds to the grounds of enchantment
Came down—to the margin of waters;
And fishes came up to the lilies,
So charmed by the rapturous singing.
Love shown in the blush o' the roses!
'Twas fair in the cups of the lilies!
Love caroled from bills o' the singers,

'Twas sweet in the waters of crystal!
O love, in the dew o' the morning,
And soft in the flow o' the grasses!
O love, in the cloud and the even,
That blushed to the color of crimson!
O love, in the gleaming of Venus,
And mild in the paleness of Luna!
O love, in the soul o' the woman
Who loved so the love of "a dreamer!"

II.

O God! oppositions of forces!
They make the wild, turbulent plunging
Of torrents and swirling tornadoes!
The maiden saw not as her parents.
They said I was "only a dreamer!"
Because—Oh! when I remember,
My old, timeworn spirit doth tremble
Again with a storm of rebellion!—
Because I had loftier yearnings
Than cramping *all* thoughts to the getting
Of money by tricks of the trader—
Because I unburdened my spirit
Of some of its plungings of passion,
And tenderer play of emotions,
In figures of speech and in sonnets,
They said to me, cold as the iceberg:
"Foolish youth, you are only a dreamer.
Do you deem the invention of figures

Of speech and of amorous verses
Is enough for the fairest of women?
Why, YOU are as clumsy as dock-leaves,
While she is as graceful as lilies—
Shall lilies lock arms with the dock-leaves?"

I ventured to answer, not mildly:
"Nay, nay! but the dock, so uncomely
Yet strong, may lean over the lily,
Protecting from sun and the tempest!"

Far better I never had spoken!
For red as the raging of wine-cups,
He cried: "Let the bottom be riven
From under the dashing Vermilion!
Let clouds that are red in the even
Turn dark as your tawny complexion!
If ever so clumsy a dreamer,
Unpolished, shall wed my Eulalie!
You may level the loftiest mountain,
You may dry up the springs of the ocean,
But *this* lies beyond your endeavor—
Go!—go from her future existence!"

III.

Yea, lives may begin soaring upward
Delighting a thousand beholders,
As rings rise in smoke toward the sunbeams—
Ascending, so soon to be broken—

To be broken, as rings of our smoking
Are broken on merciless tree-tops :
Yea, hearts may turn sad, until ripples
Of gayness sink dead 'neath the waters
And the surface that rippled in sunshine
Lies turbid o'er bodies of dead men.
But a will that is utterly broken
Or bent for the arrows of curses,
While the heart still unbroken is glowing
With rashness and poisonous passions
Is the worst of all bitterest sorrows.
There are wills that are stronger than iron,
But more may be bended as pewter—
There are wills with a seeming of beauty,
But godless as glasses of Bacchus ;
There are wills that can never be broken,
But wound, as a twine on the finger.
Why chant to the hurrying people?
Why clang to the pitiless pavement
Steps driven by wills that are stormy ?
A sound in the heart of the marble
Rings back, "it is resolute battle—
Stern war with the all that ennobles !"
And big lights that gleam in the windows
Of men of the world, how they glimmer !
" We hate thee ! we hate the emotions,
The yearnings and brazen ambitions
Of humble men, daring to battle
For thrones of exalted opinions
And characters grander than temples !"

IV.

We parted—as others have parted;
And Earth put on garments of mourning.
She said, as I turned to go from her:
"Searle, stand like a man! It is sorrow
That bridges the way to the fullness
Of power and the goal of our being!
Searle, go! you are going forever!
I shall follow your footprints, aye, always;—
Shall glide like a shadow in mourning,
Along the forsaken Vermilion,
Forsaken of you—and its sweetness.
Be strong—love, farewell!" — Thus she vanished,—
As pale as the snow in the mountains.
To me the delights of Vermilion
Turned dead as the rocks of the desert—
Turned dead as our hopes; and an angel
In black led me out of the valley,
And swung a sword over the gate-way.
I crushed with the hammer of will-power,
The thing we call "lonely!" and turning
I set my face westward from Eden.

IN LOS ANGELES—*To Esther.*

Delightful, sunny City of the Angels,
  So canopied with dewy, mellow blue,
And sentineled with mountains as evangels,
  In majesty and royal robed in hue!

Yet thou, dear one, more winsome unto me
  Than distant, beauteous holy angels are,
Art far—yet nestling near! Afar from thee?
  So far! So nestling near, thou one so far!
So far? Yea, but so near, my light, my cheer,
I must be glad, I cannot find a tear.

I see the stars gleam o'er Sierra's face,
  And think of thy most matchless wonder-eyes!
I see the slopes enflowered with blushing grace
  Which move like flowing colors 'neath the sky
Of loyal blue; then, Queen, I muse of thy
Sweet face, whose modest, chasing colors vie!

I read the book—late opened in thine eyes—
  The struggling years, with sorrow's pencil-
      tracing;
I read thy shrinking from me—*as it dies!*
  Then see thy trust gleam from thy soul's
      encasing!

I read thy love's arising from its ashes
Of hopeless times, to send its sacred flashes
   Down thro' my musing soul! O how they
      glow!
Expelling every shadow, every tinge of woe.

I see thee standing by; I see thy love-charged
      gaze;
   Thy smile; thy tear; thy drooping lashes;
      parted lips;
Thy lifted, trustful look; thy sweet amaze!
I feel thy hand-press—tendriled finger-tips!
Thy presence o'er me swings, about me clings—
Fills all my heart, and soothes its sorrowings;
Kisses my heart to peace; and sweetly sings
   Thy beauteous voice thro' all my spirit's way!
   I hear thee sing to me, I feel thee pray—
   So, tho' afar thou'rt near to-day and aye.

My new-born life would fly to thee, would fold
   Its long-time wearied wings in blissful rest
In thy heart's treasure-room more rich than gold—
   E'er revel in that paradisal feast
Thy spirit-fingers spread down in its dell:
Thy love hath healed my heart! All's well!
      All's well!

I muse of thee! I write, I sing of thee!
   I pray for thee! I plead for thee, alway!
I plan for thee, and hope the best may be!
   I reach thee Esther's sceptre—give thee sway!

Though far, my queen, thou'rt near—thou'rt
  here ;
And yet I come, I fly to thee, my queen !
Heart-distance would be death, tho' hands were
  near !
  But heart-knit, e'en with Titan mounts
    between
  Their rugged crests enwrapped in snowy
    sheen,
Could never chill our warmth of tropic loves,
Nor part these holy-mated spirit-doves !

And yet, my queen, I feel this chafing strain
  Of separating miles. Glad in thy love?
Yes ; yet by distance, joy is tinged by pain.
  I long to have thee, as the wooing dove
Back to his window flies, fly to my spirit,
So long shut, opened now for thee to cheer it.

' Twere richer, sweeter joy, my queen of May,
To be beside thyself the song to say !
  To touch thy chaste and trustful love-charged
    fingers ;
  And look into thine eyes, where alway
    lingers
A hallowed something that so beams and
  blesses
And drives away my clouds with its caresses !

O how my words so struggle and so long
  To say my heart's deep thought and sacred
    feeling

Out unto thee ; they break their hearts in song,
  And yet so little of the best revealing.
Words beat, as prisoned birds, to thee to show
  The halo of my inner heart for thee.
New Esther, "whither thou goest, I would go;
  And where thou dwellest, I would ever be ;
Yea, where thou diest, there too would I die "—
Mount with thee to the same transcendent sky—
Walk th' same celestial streets with thee—the same
  Blest river by with thee ; trust the same God
  Who led us 'neath the same strange, chast'ning rod,
Thus led us thro' by His one only Name !

LAURA OF PARADISE.

Let the river flow on with the dry winds and
    heat,
Let it shimmer like silver and laugh with its
    sheen,
And her girlhood's sweet secrets soft-tonguèd
    repeat,
Let it sing to itself—let the San Joaquin;
Let it carry rich grains to a gold-giving mart—
It is nothing to Laura's disconsolate heart.

Let Sierras ascend until ready to touch
    The dim wondrous clouds of the world of un-
        knowns,
Till the stars will descend, for they love them so
    much,
    For a kiss of delights on their frosty white
        cones;
Let the snowflakes fall swift; let them circle and
    dart,—
Are they pallid as hopes lying dead on her heart?

Let the oranges glow and the citron-trees bloom,
    Let the lemons be golden, the figs over-sweet,
Yet under and over is always a gloom;

And beside her, in front of her steps flying
    fleet,
Is the echo of steps and the sound of the clod,
Hiding all but her memories under the sod.

Let the summer winds pass and the winter winds
    sigh,
  Let the blossoms blush pink, and the leaflets
    revive,
And the live-oaks spring green, and the redwoods
    tower high;
  Let the cooing soft voice of the turtle-dove give
His halcyon tribute of peace beyond price;
But paler her joy is than snow-mantled ice.

For her heart Paradisal with tropical spring,
  With a love that was more than the common
    could woo,
In its mood was attunèd to every glad string
  That reciprocal ecstasy brings to the true,
Till the envious skies snatched her lover away;
Now her sorrow attuneth all strings to its lay.

THE VALLEY OF PEACE.

Shall we strive without fruit in the struggles eternal
    For name on the earth or for purse in the hands?
We shall end in a dearth that consummeth the vernal
    Delights of the life, and the death of the lands
    Of the heart that was flowery,—now burning with
        sands.

Shall unholy ambitions aspire to be set
    In the gardens of fancy—false Edens we crown
The cool heights of life with—to drink and forget
    The bitter below, and to never go down
    Till the wildest desires in fruition shall drown?

Shall they beat a bold march with anticipate feet
    For the fancy-built Edens? With hope over-grown,
Shall they strike, to be stricken in turn, and retreat
    In despair, and fall down as the trees over-blown,—
    Lie as helpless as they and as dust-over-strown?

Shall we rush as a storm that would master the mountains,
    And pour out our blood as the clouds that are red?
Ah, the storm shall be broken to murmuring fountains
    Retreating dismayed to the lowliest bed
    In the bottom of ocean, and lie down as dead.

Can we not be content with the peace that is sweet
   In the shadows of vines over ways that are mild?
But as birds from the vines, must we fret as we beat
   Our wings to the trees that are lofty and wild
To do battle with serpent-desires indiscreet?

They shall twine us in coils strong as sinews of sin,
   And shall drag us down lower,—down lower, alas!
Than the vineyards of peace that we left; and we win?—
   But the dust of defeat and the dirges of grass
Seethed over hope-graves we shall mourn as we pass.

Oh! the fair little valley, delectable vale,
   Set full of humilities blooming in glory,
Vined over in virtues, untorn by the gale,
   That blows in high places of Earth that are hoary
   And fretted with frosts and hail-gashed until gory.

Oh! the sweet little valley, shut in from the storms
   By roses of candor with petals of splendor!
O duties so fruited with beautiful forms
   Abashing to pleasures! Oh! chastened and tender
   And holy affections—and God is Defender!

Come down from the strife in the idol high-places,
   And in from the wars on the turbulent plains.
Why look thus so long into treacherous faces?
   You only shall gain from your terrible pains
   A life that is maimed and a spirit with stains.

Would you taste of true pleasures humility-sent,
    Red jewels of Jesus have paid for the peace
That remaineth for us, and the price of content.
    They have bought you a rest that is richer than fleece
Of all glory or gold that the years may increase.

Turn back from a battle of futilest blows!
    You shall strive—but be foiled in the struggle at last.
Here Heaven has planted a perfect repose,
    Where branches are fruited with joys, and they cast
Their blossoms of love for the beds of your rest.

TWO DEPARTURES—*Tamalpais*.

While Tamalpais' fair "Sleeping Beauty" lay
  With face turned skyward and with locks to south
Disheveled veiled the sloping mountain way,
  The sun went west from Alcatraz' stern isle,
Then kissed with glowing lip the tidal mouth
Of San Francisco's mobile matchless bay
  E'er exquisitely parted with its smile—
With rosy hand then waved farewells to night,
Then swept beyond into the westward light
To revel 'mid Pacific islands bright.

So doth thy *soul*, more free, more bright than sun,
  With earthly loves, asleep in beauty, left
On Time's Tamalpais' mount-tops one by one,
  From militant and fortressed isles of earth,
  Move Godward, and, with lips aglow and cleft,
Doth kiss the tidal mouth, that lures anon,
  Of Aidenn's islèd seas of jeweled worth—
With spirit-hand then wave farewells to time,
Then wing beyond to that Elysian clime
To dwell amid its endless scenes sublime.

CITY OF THE GOLDEN GATE.

Here stand two sunlit battlements,
  The pillars of the Golden Gate.
They, many a year of olden date,
As angel-builded resting tents
Have seemed to weary, beaten ships
  Which gleamed with eyes, with griefs untold,
That gazed above stern-bitten lips—
  Dreamed o'er their loves, but gazed for gold.

A gate between of shining wave
  Swings always, always out and in.
Here feet find rest—some hearts a grave,
  And hopes fulfill, or die by sin.

And, as a mouth drilled thro' the mounts,
  It seems to breathe a breath of gold
  Out of the deep-gorged peaks that hold
Their mints of minerals and the founts
Of blessed streams, with beds of treasure
  And banks of wealth and blooming glory—
Where Nature is eternal pleasure,
  And trees are green, when Time is hoary.

And—like a large rich-laden flower
  Of gorgeous hue and deepest sweet

    Where bees crowd on with fretting feet—
The bay blooms up, with under-power,
From ocean's heart of trembling blue;
    And men crowd on its restless rim,
Where steeples tower and banners flow,
    And sunny winds float sound of hymn.

The city of the Golden Gate—
    Shall she be built a grand and fit
    Metropolis? Or she forget
The Builder of all good and great,
    Till He shall strike His fiery hand
Beneath the proud magnificent
    And sink her streets of hollow sand—
And sea-swirl lull her discontent?

Shall she become the dream fulfilled
    Of Poe's fantastic poetry—
    Become "The City in the Sea?"
And ocean tread the iron-willed?
And rocks rise up in wrath and close
    The eye-entrancing Golden Gate,
And leave it to a strange repose,
    Or winds' and sea-waves' long debate?

SHASTA.

Amid clear chanting waterfalls, and 'mid
   The silent listening and enchanted pines,
Beneath whose stately, manly size are hid,
   Like nestling children, beauteous shrubs and
       vines—
Strong-natured pines upon the slopes arranging
   In amphitheatred, encircling lines,
Eternal list'ners to the ever-changing,
Yet ever-changeless, chanting waterfalls
With flowing, ebbing, sounding, whisp'ring calls.

'Mid forest shades beneath that wonder sky
   Of mountain California with her sun
That never clouds, I lift my eager eye
   Across the laughing, leaping sun-spots as they
       run
Athro' the shadows round me super-fair—
Creep thro' the shrubs, climb up the vines in air—
In gentle swiftness lest themselves they lose
'Mid sun-browned shadows' dusty-footed shoes.

Thus looking out beyond this singing world
   About my musing, 'trancing place of rest,
Behold! A looming, luring vision set impearled
   Upon the heaven of blue, eternal, blest,

Beams Shasta glorified, pure pearl of white;
More grand than Mars, more bright than Venus'
    light.
Olympus dwindles 'neath thy flashing glories,
As shrink, in manhood, childhood's wonder-
    stories.

But chosen words are but as smoke and dust
    That dim the splendors one would thrust to
        view—
But as the sins of men before the vision thrust
To taint the whiteness of the great white throne
    of God,
    Or shrink its grandeur—mar the snow-white
        hue :
Shall words rush in where angels meekly trod?

SACRAMENTO VALLEY IN SPRING.

With oaks of never-fading green
   And banks of changing green and brown
   And, like the very stars come down,
Strown yellow-bloomed, and set between
With every hue that sky hath seen!

Old live-oaks, tressed with mistletoe
   Uncombed, unclipt, and old as they,
   Beneath whose shades the blossoms play,
While sweet winds make the new buds blow
And sparkle in the morning glow!

Thus Sacramento in her bloom
   And Nature's rhapsody of spring,
   When love and beauty smile and swing
Their scenes and censers of perfume
Below Sierra's snowy plume.

IN THE DESERT—OVERLAND.

Overland! The sterile lands,
How they glitter in the eye!
While the hot airs stand and shimmer,
As a million spirit-wands,
With their hot and blinding glimmer,
Till the only thought is—*dry!*

Sand and sun—and sun and sand!
Till the heart is skeptic guessing
Why this desolation spread!
Why the sun the sands should wed,
With no single child of blessing—
With but sultry winds to whirl them,
And the whirlwind sent to swirl them?
Ah! we cannot understand!

Skeletons on ways of sands!
Lo! the pale clouds, overdrifting,
Go up higher, as forever
Shunning their eternal sifting—
Clouds up-reaching their thin hands,
As imploring: "Blue skies, never
Leave us to this sandy shifting,
And its breath of burning fever!"

Sand between two fertile strands—
O, how like the broken-hearted ;
Sand between two holy lands,
Land of age and youth departed !
Out from youth's green garden hurried
Still-born hopes with folded hands
Are by sands of dead faith buried.
God, we yield ! we may not know
All the sweetness born of woe !
Who shall say, though desert-worried,
If this desolate repose
May not blossom as the rose.

HUMBOLDT LAKE.

Here it lies in silentness,
  Lonely in a lonely waste,
Banks of sand and alkali—
Silent till the thoughts oppress—
  Smooth as pavements marble-faced,
Smooth and colored as the sky.

One lone dwelling on its beach,
  One lone bird, with note nor word,
Drifting, as if naught to choose,
Despondently and out of reach!—
  Leave this listless, lonesome bird—
This strange mirage of dancing hues!

THE RANCHER'S STORY.

The ranchman rose, and began to pace,
As a thought danced over his grizzled face,
And said, with much more force than grace :

Wall, an' I'll say my say, fur the reason why
  That it is my turn, it is, an' I
Must say mine afore ol' Haller 'ill tell—
  And thet is the reason fur why,
An' not ez that I am any yer swell,
A takin' a sorryful tale-tellin' spell.

Wall, to be short, then, it wuz a ranch ;
  An' ranches they waren't ez thick
Them times ez now they be. 'Twas down on a branch
  O' the Brazos—you've been on the very spot, Rick—
And the rancher he waren't so wealthy ez I—
The one I'm a speakin' uv—this uz the reason fur
    why :

He wuz suthin' o' polish, or suthin'
  Uv sich like a word that book-men say, ez I've
    heerd.
There waren't no book, or no language—no nuthin'
  That he didn't know uv; so ez thet he appeared
Ez sharp as the lightnin,' an' double geared.

They sed that he "broke" in a queer kind o' way,
Once back in the East, an' atween a night an' a day
Hed to start up, wi' a patterin' heart, an' fly—
So he's poorer 'an me, thet's the reason fur why.

One thing thet be sure, thar wuz, ez I'd vote,
    The ungodliest queer-like tossin' an' start
Uv his rascalish eye ; an' I'd put up my coat,
Thar wuz suthin' stept heavy inside on his heart
In the tenderest places—but thet's neither you nor I !
Fur it's out o' the subjic', an' thet's the reason fur
    why.

He wuz poorer, an' yet he wuz richer ez me ;
    Leastwise none o' us ranchers cud buy the chap out.
For he had one lump o' treasure, you see,—
    A treasure, you see, ez would put to the rout
Yer millions uv gold an' ranches ; and thet
Wuz a bright little girl ; an', you bet,
Thar waren't no thing—'cept God—cud get
Thet gay leetle blossom, an' thar waren't no use fur to
    try—
An' so he wuz richer ez me ; *thet's* the reason fur why.

God kept her a-livin' a time, ez mebbe he might
    Meller the hard man's heart, perhaps.
    But God wuzn't going to let her to stay
Till she grew so old ez to hev the same hard way.
So, when the years begin to grow to thet pint, a blight
    Gets up an' out o' the Brazos, an' taps
Et the rancher's door ; an' the darlin' she let's it in

So it eats et this jew'l o' this man o' sin
Till she grows ez slim an' thin-limbed ez a pin—
  Till she bended down, ez a withery blossom stem,
  An' her faced dipped down i' the dust o' the earth,
  Ez the flower on the tip o' thet stem, the same!
So thar another burden o' dirt wuz throwed on his
    box o' mirth.

Then he soiled his knees wi' the dust thet wuz cover-
    in' her;
  An' he used to say: "O the clouds hang low!
And my life's as a wall, and the clouds be big wi'
    myrrh,
  And they break on my life, as a wall; and so
  They run so low they keep a-breaking, and oh!
  Baptizing it over wi' myrrh as bitter as woe!"

Then he stole her up, an' gathered her up an' burned
His jew'l to ashes—they say—an' urned
The same! Then, ez a ghost, he vanished away.
Now, I reckon he's somewhar bearin' his urn to-day!
Wi' that same tossin' about of his eye
Which nobody knows the terrible reason fur why.

THE ISHMAELITE.

I.

A cloud to east in upper air
  Was dipping from the boiling sea
  Her golden waves.   It bent its knee
And dipped, and lifting, unaware,
Some oversplashed its cup and fell
  And flashed afar a lightning flash,
And sounded with the distant swell
  Of thunder, with its hoarse-toned plash.

II.

"Wild Bill" and I 'mid seas of grass—
  And I a roaming rhymer, then,
  And he a wildest waif from men—
He, dreaming of a shattered glass
Of golden beauty, in the days
  When love and confidence, a-bloom,
Lined all his heart's perfumèd ways,
  Now sered to wasted ways of gloom.

III.

"O, gold-eyed stars!" Wild Bill began,
  "That smile one thing and wink another
  (In this far, man is false-eyed brother),

If men have found a fellowman
The world may trust, as trusting woman,—
  That *all* may trust in suns or thunders,
I'll waive my strife and turn to human,
  And add one to the seven wonders.

IV.

"Men say I spurn the very thought
  Of any throbs of heart that beat
  What woman's tongue pronounces sweet.
They may not see the sombre spot,
Encased in rocky, froward souls,
  Where love may weep in tears of weakness—
Ours woe controlled, theirs joy controls;
  Their love a boon, and ours a bleakness.

V.

"Aye, you are young; and poets know
  The meaning of a plaintive story—
  Can drop tears on a hand, though gory
And desperate—well be it so,—
I laugh with those who jest at love,
  And build a room more, with the rest;
Yet, deep within, the soul will move
  With curses at the hollow jest.

VI.

"If, in some mood of inspiration,
  You thrust my secret into rhyme,

I charge you keep it until Time
Shall fix my grave for decoration.
It may be turned to fruitful warning
   To whom would go the way I've gone—
May save my memory some its scorning.
   When all but this is overgrown.

VII.

" My distant Mary was a blonde,
   A pale face mellowed by some care
   Unusual, so finely fair.
And I, somehow, have never found
   A face, an eye, or sunny hair,
   A heart, a head, or limbs, or breast,
Or love, or goodness could compare
   With hers, divinest, loveliest!

VIII.

"The birds were thicker in the trees,
   And sat and twittered unafraid
   When she was there; and, when she prayed,
All Nature seemed upon its knees;
And rich bees, overladen, came
   And clustered on her clasping hands;
And tall-topt flowers, with hearts aflame,
   Tipped to her cheeks as charmèd wands.

IX.

"Her song was like the melody
   Poured liquidly along the keys

Of some piano in the skies—
Like some angelic symphony
That glideth, on its wings of bliss,
   Along the glittering '*glassy sea*;'
For nothing bears so pure a kiss
   Of Heaven as music's melody.

X.

"She sang one time—and, Oh! her voice!—
   While shining with a glance divine
   Her blue-blue eyes did overshine
The splendor of the sky apoise!
Rude bearded men look up and weep,
   And rough brown hands and brawny arms
Lift up and swing, and young folks leap,
   Run wild at its melodious charms.—

XI.

"And (as the tides rush to the moon),
   A thousand waking sympathies
   Rush up to kiss her melting eyes!
And strong men, rising one by one,
Unthinking, crowd and weep and lean
   Like leaning ships; and children shout
And mingle in the magnet scene,
   And white-haired men bow heads devout.

XII.

"Then I was but a lad, and yet
   Was wise in feelings that to me

Were more than all beside ; and she,
Too wise and faithful to forget.—
Some said : ' But *she* is rich in purse,
    And soon will scorn *him*, poor and humble!'—
God ! crush that heart-consuming curse,
    That block of gold o'er which fools stumble!

XIII.

"Be sure I was not rich; but then
    I had a turn of mind that many
    Count better than a soulless penny—
A buoyant soul that most of men
Would give a fortune to possess.
    They called me '*wild*'—I knew not why;
But then I made this 'off-hand' guess:
    To make me odious in *her* eye !

XIV.

"Thank God, I was not dull or tame;
    For Mary could not love a drone,
    Nor worship hearts of gold or stone—
I was not wild nor tame, I claim.
Could God then love me aught the less,
    Because I claimed the right of motion ?
There was no form 'twixt heart and cross,
    Nor stupidness in my devotion.

XV.

"But still they called me 'wild,' the same—
    Ah ! *then* it made me weep : such tears

Have long since perished with the years—
I glory in the ruffian name.

*   *   *   *   *

One Rudolph came, a moneyed drone,
   Who claimed (by right of unearned gold
And by the right that parents own)
   Their *offered* child—*a slave is sold!*

XVI.

"Her parents loved him for his riches,
   And tried to sell her to a drone—
   'She asked for bread; they gave a stone!'
They sewed a veil with golden stitches,
And thought to hide from her the boy
   Whose cupid had no golden arrow—
They thought a little golden toy
   Would turn her from her bitter sorrow.

XVII.

"Now, what if minted silver shine
   And rattle in the purse and chink
   In chests chained down by diamond link?
What if the burden of a mine
Of minted gold should pouch and weigh
   One's pockets, till the '*law*' would pass
And wink, and maidens droop, and say,
   'How rich! how grand!'—yet sad, alas!

XVIII.

"Yea, what of silver-glancing glint?
   And what of gold and glowing gilt?
   And palaces that tower and tilt
O'er wide-spread lands afar a-tint
With harvest wealth—that tower a-top
   This little tilting, toppling earth?
All these were but a trifling drop
   To satisfy a world of dearth.

XIX.

"For what were these if one must miss
   The only face, the only form,
   The only breast or clasping arm,
The only elevating kiss,
The only hand whose press or touch
   Could raise the dead heart or arouse
One slumbering joy—the only such
   To heal the heart that bleeds and bows?

XX.

"To cease to love too saintly true,
   Too fond to ever disobey
   Parental will, too frail to say:
'I will not wed, and live to rue!'
And so — Alas! — hold, till I quiet
   This stormy motion in my breast—
This damnèd lunging spirit-riot
   Of recollection—then the rest!

XXI.

"The pallor of my evil star,
  Perhaps, as cold, weird light in dreams,
  Has cast its hue in pallid streams
Before you, and its lines afar
You follow, till your thoughts unveil
  The bitter truths I strive to tell—
At which the *wildest* soul will quail,
  As demons at the wails of hell.

XXII.

"'What *God* has joined!' Those words were
    maddest.
  Had *she* been glad by his caress,
  When wed, my heart had murmured: 'Bless
The saintly flower!'—But, ah! the saddest,
I saw her when the year had flown,
  A shadow then, and sorrow-veiled,
By walks that youth with joy had strown—
  They feigned they knew not why she failed.

XXIII.

"Swift passed another year; and I
  (As was my way since she was wed),
  Went wandering (with the stars o'er head),
Where holy water glimmered by—
The deep and glinting lake, where we
  Had both breathed wishes up to God,
And I to her, and she to me—
  Now one lone flower bloomed on the sod.—

XXIV.

"One marvelous, symbolic flower;
  Too delicate to stand alone,
  It leaned against a heartless stone,
Yet exercised its fainting power
In breathing perfumed prayers to me.—
  Just then I started, for I felt
Some feeling pull me to my knee!—
  I looked! *the flower had turned to wilt!*

XXV.

"A thousand longings, resurrected,
  Rushed to the lake!—I cast my eyes
  Upon its wave-reflected skies!—
Two hands played with two stars, reflected;
One pale breast cooled upon the lake;
  One white face kissed the floating moon!—
I called!—the sleeper would not wake!—
  I cried out in the night—alone!

XXVI.

"I plunged into the star-strewn lake!—
  I clutched—'twas *she!* O silent Mary!
  Dead on the waters solitary!
The *ripples* on the lake-shore break;
But red *heart-surges* break and toss
  Her soul on billows, till the child
Through death is lifted from her cross,
  While I, tossed woeward,—yea, am *wild!*

XXVII.

"O red-winged life ! with bloody beak
   Scouring the wild plains of my heart
   To catch prey for the hungry mart
Of misery ! I was not weak :
I paid them for their godless sneers—
   No matter how.—I made them feel
The reflux of my youthful tears
   Drop back on them like frozen steel."

Since this was said, his tongue is dumb.
   His grave is fixed—for decoration ?
   Or, for neglect, or desecration ?
I know not if a friend has come
With flowers, or spray of "live-forever,"
   To honor this strange Ishmaelite :
If so, I say, God bless the giver !
   This is my flower, this song I write.

He died (some say, a desperado)
   The steadiest nerved—the coolest man
   That ever set foot on the plain—
The Hero of the Estacado.
Ah ! dare we hope, he found the flower
   That melted by the heartless stone—
And that, through God's eternal hour,
   He is not "*wild*," and not alone ?

EDGAR A. POE.

I.

Weird meteor of a doleful dye
Thus flaming in a gloomy sky,
As wayward as a comet wild,
Thou strange, romantic, unknown child,
A bust of deep unearthly woe,
Mysterious, morbid, dreamy Poe!

II.

Lamented be the day that found
Thy storm-swept vessel rockward bound;
And doubly cursed the fatal day
When thy lone lifeboat shattered lay
In floating fragments o'er the sea!—
A mournful loss when Heaven lost thee!

III.

Thou wast an angel strayed to earth,
Thy voice commingling with the mirth,
And dreaming, not of gloom, but joy
And Heav'n and beauty, fair-haired boy:
But "*fallen!*" what a word of wail!
What ranks of anguish crowd its trail!

IV.

Who knows the swelling veins of gall
That rent thy soul when thou didst fall?
Who knows the quenchless flame that fired—
Consumed thy peace, and then expired
And left the evil all unburned—
The ashes of thy soul unurned?

A DIRGE.

Talk low; it is done,
His love-hope is dead.
Go, lay it alone;
Its glory is fled—
Go, bear it as one
Bears—sorrowful tread!—
Dead longings in lead.

The bud that was fair
Will never be bloom;
'Tis covered in brown
Leaves, dead as despair,
Slain by its own gloom—
Leaves dead and dropped down.

The star is gone over—
Is set in the sea,
Which gloometh, where hover
Ill-bodings to me!
The star, as the clovers
Swirled under the dust,
Rolls under the tosst
Sea, cold as dead lovers,
And pale as a bust.

The cheek that was red
Is paler than shrouds—
Is colder than lead!
The beauty of dawn,
Black-veiled in the clouds
Of mourning, is gone!

NOLETHA.

I.

Soul of Noletha, could I grasp
    The echo of a whisper only!
Soul of Noletha, could I clasp
    Thy hand that reaches lonely, lonely!
Despair stings sharper than an asp!
    Soul of Noletha, let us swear
    Eternal hope against despair!

II.

Soul of Noletha—Soul of Love,
    Impearled eternally within
A passion purple as above
    God's purple skies—as chaste of sin!
I feel some promise, knit of love—
    A love deep-visioned as the seers—
    That joy will bloom yet from our tears.

III.

My heart! illusions lure thy hope
    To lose the savor of its reason;
We *must* go mourning as we grope
    Thro' never-changing wintry season.
Why shuffle thoughts with glowing trope

So oft, so long—O Love, how long?
No answer rights the seeming wrong.

IV.

I feel so strangely overcast—
  So burdened by the catching breath
Of some invisible and vast
  Angel of something twin to death,
The wish across my spirit passed
  Alone, alone my soul to weep
  Itself away to God's sweet sleep.

V.

If but a word could leave the ark
  That floats thy spirit—yea, one word—
And flutter through the floods of dark,
  Tho' but an instant to be heard,
'Twould be like music of the lark
  Arising to my mounts of snow
  To break their solitudes of woe!

VI.

If but thy finger, charged with love,
  Could touch me, its magnetic power
Might yet electrify and move
  The fainted, fallible soul-flower
To lift its face the snows above;—
  Noletha,—no, 'tis but my fancy
  That cheats my mind with necromancy.

VII.

Go back, O heart! Thy weird retreat
    Can shield thee from the eyes without!—
Conceal thy secret, wrapped in sleet,
    And fold thy mem'ries close about
To cover love with robes discreet;
    And, Levite-like, the world will pass
    And *falsely* say "Thy soul is brass."

THAT DREAMLESS SLEEP.

A SONG FOR LIFE.

I.

We muse, in measured tones of woe :
  "O for the deep and dreamless sleep!"
Then smile an interlude of "No!"—
  "Ah, Life, delusion-crowned and steep,
I choose the silent rest below!"
  We sing, but break the rhyme to leap,
To looming peaks, illusive-bright,
Then chafe to rise to loftier height.

'Tis easy uttered in the light;
  'Tis easy spoken in the play,
But well repented of, when night
  Suggests the darkness and decay—
The hollow silentness and blight,
  When we are still and put away—
Yea, then we fear, and cry: "Forgive!
Repeat, O years, repeat, and live!"

II.

Lone, like a single stem of wheat
  Left leaning o'er a headed field,
And, bending with untimely heat,

A queenly chastened woman kneeled,
And paled to hear herself repeat
  That wish—few hearts have ever sealed;—
We chant it sunward on the breeze,
Then pray: "*Be broken in the trees!*"

Her child, the seal of peaceful love,
  Had melted in the breath of God
And flown, like incense sweet above;
  And friends had fallen to the sod—
Left her to grieve a mateless dove,
  In ways of night all newly trod;
She moans above her dead delight,
"I die! I fly beyond this night!"

But words are like alluring signs
  That tell not *all*, or tell amiss,
The thoughts within the secret lines;
  And grief may picture signs of bliss,
As bliss may seem to bloom in wines—
  And, when the pale god came to kiss
The white seal on her lifted brow,
She thrust it back—"Not now! Not now!"

The dead face of a love may stare
  Away the quiet of the breast;
The dead kiss of a child may wear
  Away the lips of early rest.
Now days of grief to her are fair,
  For, while her life swings in the West,
The hours go up with shining wings
Sweet with the "song for life" she sings.

III.

With purpose stronger than the oaks,
  And aspirations tall as pines
Above the mountain-crowning rocks—
  With wits that shone as diamond mines—
With fine-cut face, Adonis locks,
  A youth broke through the twining vines
Of young affections, into strife,
Which, won, is pain—which, lost, is life!

He ran the labyrinthine way
  Of learning swift as love in youth,
He rose!—He fell—aye, in a day!—
  Those hearts he sacrificed in ruth;
His rude deeds to the heads of gray;
  His subtle dodges with the truth;
Deserted friendships, whose frank eyes
Ran tears of blood from broken ties;—

These deeds hung on him, ill-voiced seers,
  As dry leaves on the dying oak,
And rustled their eternal jeers.—
  He watched the going up of smoke,
And dared to utter, through his fears;
  "Take up the life ambition broke!
The smoke ascends and melts in peace—
Thus, life, like incense, finds release!"

Then night poured down the way he trod;
  In midnight dusk and silvery light,
The moon gleamed like an eye of God;

And, like angelic eyes by night,
A thousand stars shone out abroad—
  And moon and stars, with glistening might,
Seemed searching out his covered thoughts
And frowning on his coward plots.

His heart strikes weary fists with fate,
  Which beats it till it bleeds, and he
Goes down beneath the ruthless weight,
  Like tents beat down upon the lea—
And then he calls, "Unlock death's gate!"
  And loudly knocks—"Swing back for me!"
But, when ajar, how quick to cry:
"Swing shut! quick, quick! I will not die!"

IV.

We look up at the happy stars,
  That shed like gleams of peace their beams;
We look in on the thousand scars
  And pangs of heart, then speak in dreams,
Not all of sleep — "Death end these wars
  Which keep us from pacific streams
That wind yon star-delightsome land!"—
Then wake and tremble where we stand.

Then wake and tremble that we dared
  To dream of parting hands with dust,
Till dust should more than be impaired—
  Should fall in pieces fine as rust;
And few have then so far despaired

That they could lay the crumbled trust,
With no regret, to whence it came—
Could welcome what our dreams declaim.

V.

Flowered in the splendor of her youth,
   And tossed by every balmy stir,
Of atmospheres of spring and truth,
   More fair than all fair things that were,
Unscarred by any touch of ruth,
   And unembittered by the myrrh
That comes to many maidens, she
Was won to love's dear rhapsody.

The snows flowed down; the flowers came up;
   The birds went over; golden bees
Dug in their mines, and bore their cup
   And bars of gold; and summer seas
Went on, as stars came down to sup—
   Still smiling at his winsome pleas
And, playing in the meads of pleasure,
She moved to love's redundant measure.

Go over, birds; and, gold-winged star,
   Come down to sup; and, seas of fame,
Come in; and, bees, bear cup and bar
   Of gold; and flowers, arise and flame—
Another came her joy to mar
   Who won her lover; hence she came
To seek the river's deadly pall,—
But shrank, and clasped this life of gall!

Sing not of those, whose spirits stray
  Insanely through a fancied night!
They of a frenzy plunge away—
  No logic plans, but pangs and blight
Have sprung the balance; so that they
  Are worse than dead, and have no might
To will for life or death ;—'tis these
That fall by self, the shattered trees!

VI.

When friends have passed the silent door,
  And loves, as birds through broken panes,
Have flown, but left their spots of gore,
  We sit among those darling stains,
And say: "'Tis done! I strive no more!
  Shut down the blinds! The best of gains
Is rest of rests!"—We whisper low,
Then meet the echo with our, "No!"

VII.

In keen, illusive action taught
  We wind our life into a ball—
As acrobats, then toss the thought
  As one would toss a thought of gall—
So wildly tossed,—yet shrewdly caught.
  We feign—yet fling it but to fall
Back to the hands that hurled it fro,
Then kiss the Life we feigned to throw.

VIII.

My lamp looks in my weary eyes,
   And seethes its sorrowful complaint,
And seems to call in endless sighs;
   "Turn down the wick! I burn in vain!"
But, when I would, it strives to rise,
   And flares its wish to burn again;
"Turn down the Life!" 'tis swiftly sighed,
   Then swift repented, and denied.

IX.

O Love, thou wild, ungoverned god!
   Thou rude executor of lives!
Uncertain plowing human sod—
   With keenest of all pruning knives
Cutting our piece off bud by bud!
   Thy blood-plashed plow, it drives and drives
Its red share thro' the roots of soul
Uprooting every cherished bole.

Yea, who can break that power, that breaks
   A million hearts, and yet can smile;
And peaceful sleeps, and joyful wakes—
   A million more hearts leads to guile,
To where the light of hope forsakes.
   I saw one join that sombre file
Of those who bear the tarnished urns
Of dusts of peace—that ne'er returns.

She died not quick, as day goes down,
   Nor quick as flowers that droop by frost;

THAT DREAMLESS SLEEP.

As California's April-grown
    Luxuriant grass half blossom-lost,—
She slowly died; as it turns brown
    By summer drought, and dust embossed,
Returns to dust. Her pallid face
Death crowded graveward space by space.

But even *she* looked back to earth,
    And yearned for years. They were not much
To such as she; and yet their dearth
    Was worth her wish. Ah! worth the touch
Of beads of prayer,—"Tho' void of mirth,
    Let speed the steed of life; for such
Is better than the breathless bed
Where I must sleep, when I am dead!"

And, when she fell, as shivered bust,
    Down from the saddle, in the race,
Her last words were: "Yea, God is just;
    But, oh! to lie with upturned face,
Yet see no skies—! Lie in the must
    And chill of that deep breathless place!—
Oh! let me stay with life and sorrow,
At least, till one more sweet to-morrow!"

And, when her voice had died to rest,
    In all the agonies of signs,
She cried for life!—It may be best,
    We dread to drop the slender lines
So still ride on, though sable-dressed,
    And cling to life, as clinging vines,

And, when we crumble, stir our dust
To transient life, to plead for "trust."

X.

Like pictures on the silent walls,
    We hang our lives, then turn to leave ;
When, hearing something in the halls,
    We fear some ghosts, we would deceive,
Are stealing in with secret palls
    To take the lives we seem to grieve—
We turn and seize them quick with trembling
And own the truth we were dissembling !

XI.

We plan to sparkle like the dew—
    To sparkle through an hundred years—
To sparkle like the splendid few
    Sweet drops that crown the upper spears ;
But, learning, all too soon and true,
    That those which lie unseen, as tears
We never shed, outlive the rest,
We fall to common lots at best;

To getting grain, and garments spun
    Enough for needs; and take to ease!
We rise not in the beating sun;
    We take to shadows of the trees.
We turn from all we might have won
    To hammocks swung in healthful breeze
And grateful choose a life discreet,
Where death comes with belated feet.

So loves may die; and hearts may break;
   And fortunes sink, as vain as dust;
And forms may sleep, to never wake—
   Come all things that may wear or rust,
Or life can give, or life could take,
   We beg of Nature longer trust,
Before we pay the debt, whose claim
Takes all, except the chiseled name!

Come back, then, years that sorrow stole!
   Come back, O days that folly slew!
Come back, O Life, too near the goal!
   The deeds against thee, Life, undo!
O Life, unroll the wrinkled scroll!
   Come back, O Life, we would be true—
We love thee well—would give all things,
Ere thee, O Life, with speeding wings!

A DOUBLE PROPHECY.

The amethystine sky of youth, grown cold,
Is not so brilliant purple as of old.
I see much farther through the ways of men—
Can read much deeper through the murky fen
Of reckless motives of the worried world
With sweet deceptions brightly crown-impearled—
Can better make interpretation through
The touch of human hands, if they be true
Or false in touch—can see a pallid grief
Hid 'neath the flowers and grasses of a laugh—
Can analyze a tear, if it be sweet
Or bitter fallen — aye, am more discreet
In unaspiring ways of earth, so fleet.
No thought of God so pure, so high, so deep,
But I could feel it with the finger tip
Of boyish faith, and touch the gems, and smile
With expectation, in some better while,
To wear a crown beset with those sweet pearls—
To promise *better* to such youth unfurls
A field of joy indeed! The leaves, unshut,
In image of some truth, some bliss, seemed cut
With diamond of God's finger; and the streams
Poured o'er the tongue of Nature like sweet dreams
To God's great sea of wisdom, from whose bank

I made my daily voyages, and drank
The boundless waters of the sea. The stars,
I plucked them sparkling from my ship's still
    spars.
There was no spirit storm, within, without,
Could sink them in the sea of sky—no doubt
Could stir its waves to toss them from my grasp.
The hand of her of youthful beauty in my clasp
I held, and followed in the way her gaze
Would indicate. I dreamed they saw the ways,
That lead more near the infinite than mine.
How easy, with such dreams of the divine,
To journey up to citadels of God,
With blessings beaming on the fields we trod.
The very angels seemed to wind their fingers
Around her ringlets, as her beauty lingers,
So shimmering in the sun of love and health,
That souls are dazzled with their silent wealth.
Her tread seemed ever bearing up, and I
Strove up with her. The glory of the sky
Had well been proud of the resemblance, then,
Of her pure mellow eyes—the glowing red, again,
Been proud of kinship to the redness of
Her cheeks, where Modesty, in red, wrote
    "*Love:*"
The soul that breathed life in the universe
Could press her soul, we deemed, and not be
    worse
Polluted by her super-saintly touch—
So wild a fancy seemed not over-much.

'Twas in the Maytime, and who then had
    thought
So fair a bloom would seed so cold a lot !
My dreams were more delirious with delight
Than bubbling real. The mind, o'erleaping
    sight,
Is half a prophet ; and the things we spurn
As *superstitions* by the reeling urn
Of reason, flee by day, and re-assault
The soul by night, and pillage every vault.
We waken in the dawn—at first we weep ;
Then scorn the *superstitions* of our sleep.
To stab at love, the murder of a joy
Or wistful hope in some flower-strewn decoy
Are all pre-acted in our dreams ; and we
But laugh, and call it *fancy: So with me.*
When flowers were at their fullest, and the grass
Was emerald, and moons that slowly pass,
Bloomed brightest of the May, then stars, fair-
    tresst,
Began to tremble, falling in the west,
And toss beyond my reach—then, one by one,
Sink in the rolling, distant storm, undone.
The moon began to shake upon her stem,
Then laid her face upon the floods, that hem
Her round in whirlpools, sounding with the
    roar
Of turbulence ! And blossoms, beaten lower,
Roll, broken, down to earth, and sink away,
As stars had sunken in the surge and spray.

I could not see far up,—so gazed about
Upon the washing, wasting Earth, and thought
Of her the distant beautiful : But waves
Had swirled between us, with their dashing
    heaves
The drifts of wrecks innumerable strove
The chaos to o'erleap that round them drove.
The floods grew foul at times and roily-hued,
And clayey-thick ; and then, with waifs and
    wood,
Rushed on with fury; and in pieces piled
Their freights of ruin at my feet with wild
Impetuosity ! I wailed aloud !
But waves so seething with the battering crowd
Of wrecks confused, outspoke my utterance !
And then a crested surge tossed in my glance
My soul's own beautiful, its worshiped *love !*
And *she* is struggling in the sea, and swiftly
    drifting
Beyond my reach forever ! And is lifting
Her hands for help to *One* who stands, in pride,
And leans to take her from the maddened tide,
To shores afar and opposite from mine !
"O heart beyond, you win my all, 'tis thine !"
I called in pain, then woke : it was a dream.
I wakened with the *superstition* deep
Upon the soul ; then shook the myths of sleep
Away from me ; and from the troubled brain
I combed the superstition, with its pain,
With those electric teeth of laugh:—Then ran

To meet my—*nameless!* . . .
But she had wed chill Death with brow a-frown!
An avalanche of snows had slidden down
Upon me in one night; and all the glow
And glory of the mount and vale, by woe,
Had shriveled in one night. I cast my eyes
Up toward the former amethystine skies—
They hung a broad and ebon coffin lid,
Too mighty, by my frailty, to be slid,
Or lifted, and too hard to penetrate,
To flee the room so sombre desolate.
And so I could but turn to common ways
Or sinking deeper in the treacheries
And lower wisdom of this wary world.—
Leaves now seem handkerchiefs of Nature, hurled
Or shaken in my face in mockery;
And I have wandered from those streams that flee
In flowing melody to Wisdom's sea;
And dust from fruitless digging still on-worries
      me—
The dust from groveling mines of grumbling
      men,
From which sometimes I would aspire again.

    *   *   *   *   *

Then thoughts of love's luxuriance, I bewail,
Come, in my musings, and convert the frail
And flickering spirit fire, I set aflame,
To burn instead the sun that set, when came
The superstition turned to dreary real—

Come and convert these memories I feel
Into the image of that sun of May,
Forgetting, I bask in its fancied spray.
My chamber walls of pallor cold and stern,
To skies of amethyst, in splendor, turn!
Again stars hang in th' window, and I reach
To handle them again, then start—and preach:
"'Tis but a *superstition!*" o'er and o'er
"'Tis but a *superstition!*" Wake no more
To call it fancy; heart declares it *real!*
I dream and say that time will yet reveal
Our dreams and reveries as deepest truth—
The prophets of our active lives!—I see
This remnant of my hope *that this day-revery*
Doth *prophesy* that time will yet *redeem*
What *vanished* with *fulfillment of a dream.*

ESTHER.

I.

The days unevenly fly over, Esther,
In jagged flocks of unforgetful years—
Some low and sorrowful as in disaster;—
Some higher longings carry as the condor;
And still the green upon my spirit seres,
As withereth the grasses, in the autumns, under
The southward-soaring flocks; and still the wonder
Is that thine arrow, buried in my tears,
Fresh woundeth still tho' far that *"Early Yester"*

II.

Sometimes a hundred birds go over, Esther,
And never win my never-resting eye;
Then one small note may prove a strong requester,
And marvel eyes will suddenly be lifted
And follow them along the yellow sky,
Until the last one silent-sad has drifted
A-down the gloaming distance, then I sigh,
Thus, far are flown my hopes of *"Early Yester."*

III.

Sometimes a lone bird worries over, Esther,
And winds unfriendly beat, and beat it back,

And so it flutters earthward from the bluster,
And, silent-grieving as a thwarted rover
Who chafes, if *forced* to bend his zigzag track,
Hangs, tempest-baffled, stationary over.
So (O my deepest worshiped, wayward lover)!
Storm beat and weeping through its veil of black,
I seem to touch heart to that "*Early Yester.*"

IV.

And so the birds go on and over, Esther,
As solemn days string over into years;
Still new the memory of that disaster,
And all the word from back of *me* is "*never!*"
The while the green within my spirit seres;
And all the utterance from o'er the river,
Tho' mystical, is clear to me, "*dissever!*"
And all my answer is the threaded tears
That string a-down the path to "*Early Yester.*"

TO ESTHER.

God set a clock up in my heart; it standeth
And measureth my wayward hours of living.
It ran, long time, so fitful by the heaving
Unrest of one sweet, boyish, broken passion.
I said (God knoweth well what motive so commandeth):
"Doze on, my heart! 'tis not worth while believing
A dream—'tis but my unforgetting fashion!"

And so—I heard it, thro' my years of slumbers,
Tick tenderly and measuring my yearnings,
Tong mellowly my hourly heart-returnings
Unto the hilltop of my early passion;
While morning fire of boyhood died to embers,
And I dozed on, nor rose to keep its burnings—
O love, forgive me! 'twas my wayward fashion.

It was my fashion—until at the setting
Of yester's sun—the tender and the mellow
Were drowned eternal in the sudden billow
Of an alarm tumultuous loud with passion
That God had set before begun regretting,
To go off when sweet, distant-parted Esther died
   —and yellow
Hang leaves to-day, that yester-morn hung green
   'mid bloom of fashion!

So is the way. We grow up as the bushes
That balmy south winds blow two tops together ;
Their lip-leaves kiss—their branch arms woo
    each other,
So float they in the May with warm and pleasant
    passion,
Till suddenly the wind wheels northward, and
    the blushes
Of leaves and flowers steal off, and they, aged by
    the weather
Of griefs, are blown to other mates—so is the
    fashion.

The one then nearer to the cold wind's blasting
Dies earlier, and God sets off that crashing
And loud alarm, that starts the other dashing,
Wild with the anguish of his hidden passion,
Thro' his short lane of life ! Thus seems God's
    casting.
Our weak eyes cannot read this mystic flashing,
Yet God knows best—His is a perfect fashion !

MY FAR-AWAY.

I.

O link of love ! O lifted eye,
    Impassioned girl, my "Far-Away!"
Expectant song of "by-and-by,"
    Glad yester-morn but sad to-day !
My soul stands up and looks afar
And trembles like a straying star
And reaches back, with eyes ajar,
To thee, my joy, my "Far-away."

II.

O voice, a-reel with wines of song
    More fond and fine than foam or spray
That can from vines of earth be wrung,
    Sing marches for my feet to stray
Somewhere that sin may not betide,
And streams of youthful thought beside—
Beside thy soul temptation-tried
And found so true, my "Far-Away!"

III.

O eyes, beneath another sky,
    Look up now, while I look, and pray !
I am not gone so far but I
    Can catch the kind and tender ray !

There is a wire from me to thee
By way of Heav'n—I bow my knee—
Glad eyes of love, shine o'er to me
By way of Heav'n, my "Far-Away!"

IV.

O distant heart, beat on! O beat,
   And beat thy warm and darling May!
Half way to thee we seem to meet,
   And heart to heart we seem to lay.
I feel the throb of thine, I know,
By way of Him who sayeth, "Lo!
I'm with you always!"—Angel, so
I seem with thee, my "Far-Away!"

CONFIDENCE.

Untroubled, diamond confidence,
   This would I have, my priceless pearl,
That need not question whither, whence,
   Where, why, amid the changing whirl,
But, pure as gold, and clear, intense,
   Just *my* own loyal little girl.

That in thy goings and thy thought,
   Thy pleasures, pains, thy sweet desire,
By what or whom thy heart is sought,
   Thou, on thy soul's impearlèd lyre,
Shalt only feel *my* touch of finger—
   Shalt know *me* there and feel *my* gaze—
My presence always with thee linger,
   By all thy bright or cloudy ways!

To know thou standest in the light—
   That all thou art within is day,
And all thy movements diamond bright
   And open as a sunny bay—
That thou hast nothing to conceal
To know which might becloud my weal!

To *know*, if with thee, or if miles
   Stretch out their desert loneliness,
Still, lover's look, or lover's smiles,

Or touch, or voice, or saintly kiss,
Love-speaking gifts or written words
Do never flit like secret birds
   To any heart but *mine—intense*
   And clear and single confidence!

To know *thou* knowest all I know
   Concerning our dear fellowship—
To feel *I* know that thou dost throw
   Out in the search-light's glowing dip
   Thy heart and way—that, lip to lip,
We only ever feel the flow
   Of man's and woman's holy love,
   Proved truer as we ever prove!

To have thee cure this heart disease,
   Wrought in my spirit thro' the years
Of broken longings, sorrow's seas
   Of dead hopes and of leaden tears!
To cure by such o'er-mast'ring love,
Such *single love* as from above
   Might fill an angel's heart of fire,
   Or weight with love a seraph's lyre!

No woman's hand but *thine* for *me!*
   No tender folding arm but thine!
No other's love-look would I see!
   Thy kisses so my soul refine—
No other's lips shall magnetize
My nature into ecstasies!

Is this too much to give, my queen?
  Nay, had I powers of heart and mind
And charms of all e'er love has seen
  Abundant as the fire-refined
Rich Afric diamonds and the gold
  Of Incas stored, I'd give thee all,
  And cry, my queen, "''Tis all too small!"

Is this too much to ask from thee,
  My Princess, with the pearlèd crown,
Invisible to all but me
  And Christ, who, loving us, looks down?

THINE EYES.

I see thy love-enraptured fair uplifted face;
  I see thine eyes, kind, mellow as the dove's;
Inexplicable, sweet eyes, with beauteous grace
    Now toward me, glowing forth from thy hid
      loves:
Thou h'st ravished all my heart with those en-
    dearing eyes,
My sister, and my love, my queen; and by thy
    look I rise!

Rise from my loneliness, my hidden hopelessness!
  Thine eyes, my stars of hope, gleam in—my
    stars,
Like Bethlehem's sweet, sainted star, to bless;
  With healing in their beams so full the very
    scars
Are smoothèd from my soul-life, and my sighs
Melt into smiles by th' kiss of thy dear eyes.

I drink in joy their yet unpictured splendor.
  They speak to me, they smile to me, they twine
Somehow so exquisitely tender
  Like sweet seraphic fingers, Princess mine!
They fold my heart, they kiss my heart, they cling
Like Ruth. I clasp forever what they bring—

They bring?   Unutterable are what things they
    bring,
  As doves with feathers of refinèd gold
And swinging forth upon clean silver wing—
  As doves' eyes—such celestial doves, behold!
My chastened Princess' now uncurtained eyes!
"Come near, my dove, my undefiled," my spirit
    cries,
Blue-eyes, brown-eyes, Keats-emerald eyes, how
    they translate
Me out of grief to glad—give strength and make
    me great!

I bless thy springing feet, the mercy-messengers
  And beautiful; and fondle with delight
Thy clinging hand that deeds of good prefers;
  Admiring clasp thy trustful form to-night;
Thy matchless hair I twine my toying fingers
    thro';
  I love thy speaking, fair, inspirèd face;
  Thy lips impassioned, pure, pink-delicate of
    grace;
But lo! thy peerless eyes, thy violet eyes have
    won the throne
O'er all thy beauties, oh, my joy and crown, my
    own!

Yet these, I feel, I *know*, are little, May,
  So little these beside thy heart that lives
Within thy beauties, holding royal sway—

Thy heart that loves me, and so eager gives
Its hallowed sympathies and honor, praise and
love and *all*
Into my longing soul thro' these. Darling, I fall
Into thy opened heart, which quickly claspeth
me—
Anointeth now my long-unmated heart (made
free),
Out of the holy horn of your great love, as
you so sweetly sing ;
Thus, Dear, thou settest me upon thine inner
throne, to be
Thy king! thy trusted king! thine honored
king! thine own loved king!
To-day you, in your queenly heart-room, nestle
to your king, unseen, yet seen,
To-day, I, in my regal heart-room, sit beside and
clasp my queen—
Chaste queen! fair queen! sweet queen! love-
crowned heart-queen!

MY FLOWERS.

I sit among the flowers alone to-day,
And yet I am not—cannot be alone,
For, everywhere that blossoms hold their sway
In winsome dignity or sunshine play,
There ever comes my living Flower, my own,
With more than splendor of enrapt'ring flowers,
And pulsing with immortal love-born powers.

The asters, stars grown from the vivid earth,
Nod toward me, smiling with a modest sense
Of rarest worth and high nobility of birth;
But, oh! my love's bright eyes, profound, intense,
Look into mine, outshining in their look
All other stars (which swiftly pale, forsook),
And fill my look, my heart, my all with thee,
My musing, beaming May, best star to me!

Syringa swing their pure and spotless white
Above my head—o'er my once weary life—
Drop petals as the snow, yet warm as flakes of light;
"Pure, peaceable;" they say, and lull the wind-
  blown strife;
But thy pure, helpful hand swings closer to me, Love,
And, putting back syringa branches, strokes my
  cheeks,

And strews the petals of thy pure white hallowed
    peace
Upon my face and inner soul and sweetly speaks
By touch as frank, love-full as souls above ;
And *thus*, Dear Heart, my spirit-chafings cease!

Forget-me-not, so delicately blue,
Looks up and pleads, with reticence and grace,
" Come, touch my soul, enwrapt in loyal hue,
And brush my timid loneliness with *thy* strong face !"
Then opening to my keep-sake—withered? Yes, but
    true,
And vocal with a blessed, blessing memory !—
Thou, Darling, comest, with my look, and that small
    spray
Transforms to thee, thou pretty, patient May,
Transforms to thee, my true, my loyal Love—to thee
Who fillest all my vision, all my ways, my heart !
"Forget me not—forget thee not !" thus, brilliant
    Bird, thou art
Forever singing to my happy spirit ! *Thee* forget?
Seas, continents, might come between—yea, death
    might be,
But cleaves my soul to thee thro' time, thro' tides
    eternal yet.

Carnations flame my eyes before and fill
With fragrance all the arbor where I sit.
Impassioned loves seem throbbing till they thrill
The beauty-lover till it seemeth fit

Their dumb, red loveliness with mutual arms embrace !
But *thou*, warm-hearted and impassioned lover,
Dost come more close than they—bend over
My joy-o'er-flowing soul and fold thy shapely arms
About my being—press those scarlet, lip-love charms
Of thy carnation heart, and flood, in tropic kisses
As vivid as thy love, my magnet heart with passion !
That is thy strong, impulsive, loveful, chaste, sweet
    fashion !
And thus thy love is strength, protection, pureness,
    blisses,
My lily white, my pure and frank queen-lily grace ;
My aster beauty, star that never falls—fixed in my
    sky ;
My true blue Princess—my forget-me-not; and my
Carnation richness flaming such impassioned love-
    caresses ;
My joy, my light, my everything, my now and
    by-and-by !
' Mid flowers with thee I evermore would tarry,
My bright, my beautiful, my iridescent fairy.

ANNETTE.

The day was when I courted all—
I courted suns and moons and stars,
And balmy airs brimful of sounds
Of wingèd singers melodies;
I loved the clouds that hung on high
That fringed the blue and balmy sky;
I loved the fire-wheeled thunder cars;
I courted all the blooming grounds,
And courted with abundant eyes;
And all I saw enraptured me,
Because, Annette, I courted thee.

When I went wild with ecstasy
At joyous songs of mated birds
It was because, Annette, therein
Was joy—because the sound was sweet;
Not sweet because 'twas sweet,—ah, me!
'Twas sweet because it breathed of thee.
The glad bird voices were not words,
Nor tunèd to my violin,
As thine was tuned; yet they, Annette,
Were musical and chimed with glee,
As thine, when I was wooing thee.

I never dreamt, my dear Annette,
That ever any arm but mine
Could clasp thee close; I never thought

The universe another bore
Could woo my loved Annette, and yet,
Once, ere the morning star was set,
When I had breathed the final line
Whose dying notes were scarce forgot—
Ere I had more than closed the door,
Another came; I saw—I see!
That Death, Annette, was wooing thee.

Tell me, Annette, was there one night
I did not watch by thee and pray
So death, Annette, could find no time
To woo my loved one; without rest
I guarded thee. He veiled my sight;
O, starless gloom! O, dead delight!
He won my pale Annette away;
He wedded thee! How weird the chime
Of wedding bells; how white thy breast,
When thou gav'st back my ring to me
And Death, Annette, was wed to thee!

When back I gaze to-day, Annette,
I wonder how the world could blame
Our youthful love—so pure, refined.
So little doubt, so much of trust;
God knows, I never since have met,
Another love as saintly yet.
I'm not of those who love to name
Dead mem'ries o'er, nor yet the kind
To pine for what has gone to dust;
And yet my heart is not so free,
Annette, as when I courted thee.

SINCE THOU ART NOT HERE.

I.

There's a laugh in the treetop, a smile in the sky,
   And the birds with their merriment filling the glade,
And many a matron with love in her eye,
   And jollity sporting around in the shade—
But the mirth in my eye, it is courting a tear—
Tho' I smile, my heart weepeth, *since thou art not here.*

II.

The jest ringeth round in a circle of joy;
   And mine chimeth in with the chorus of laugh,
And none ever dreams of a thought to annoy
   The sweetness and gayety born, as we quaff
Such respite of care. But, alas! in their cheer,
Tho' I laugh, I am lonely, *since thou art not here.*

III.

Tho' strong is the friendship, that welcomes me home
   To the hearths of the noble and good of our land,
And tender the ties that would bid me not roam,
   And warm is their kiss and the grip of their hand,
Yet I cannot *but* roam from these ties, that are near,
While thou art far dearer, and *'way from me here.*

IV.

My heart leapeth high, as I sit by the side
   Of the fairest of sisters, companion of youth;

And her eye, like the light on the incoming tide,
  Shines up into mine with its love and its truth—
There is *peace* in her gaze, yet it bringeth a tear;
For, oh! it reminds me that *thou art not here.*

V.

There's many a maiden, too, gathering flowers,
  And throwing about me the bloom and *their smiles,*
While the gold-gilded moments string off into hours;
  Yet my fancy the *brightest* maid never beguiles
Away from *thy* flowers and *thy* smile with its cheer—
And the day groweth longer, *since thou art not here.*

VI.

And, when meditation comes on with the eve,
  And I loiter alone, in my musing I sigh.
They chide for me weeping and wonder I grieve
  With such happiness here and a Christ in the sky.
Then I go to my chamber and plead, with a tear,
That Jesus may shield thee, *since thou art not here.*

VII.

And the lamp of his love cometh down with the night,
  And I go to my rest by the light of its beams.
And my slumber is sweetened by thoughts of delight;
  And I fancy I'm with thee again in my dreams—
Which go with the morning, which comes with a tear,
And *still* I am lonely and *thou art not here.*

I MAY NOT STAY.

I.

Woman, by thy winning face,
By thy form's befitting grace,
By thine eyes of double blue,
And their tears that all-imbue
Laving thy supernal thought
Beaming through and beauty-fraught;

By thy Byron-bended lip,
Changing with emotion's trip,
By thy forehead, promise-bent,
Like a bow of wonderment,
By those hands that will not rest,
And thy never-resting breast;
By thy heart, abounding sweet,
Which would stand and never beat
Rather than it beat untruth;
By the beauties of thy youth—
By all these, and more, I pray
My unrest to let me stay!

II.

By an earlier memory,
By a face and faith and eye,
By a love I cannot give

All the beautiful that *live*,
By a dear love born to me,
By a face and form that lie
Dead to others—not to me!
By this memory of youth,
Sacred as the holy truth—
By all this, fair one, I pray
Let me go, *I may not stay!*

AGNES.

Agnes, the clouds above me
Are melted into mellow light
Beneath this magic sun, "*I love thee!*"
Love thee as the soul loves right—
Love thee as the skies of night
Love the sweet stars above thee.

Agnes, all seems to move me,
Where all ways lead me, unto *thee*.
By all my smiles, my tears I love thee;
By every bending of the knee,
By every surge of spirit's sea,
By *all* unspeakably I love thee!

Agnes, my Agnes, prove me;
But stay not, Agnes, thus so far
Barred from me, while I love thee
As the lake-tide loves its star,

Fondling on its bosom bare
Its *image* only, while above
And *distant* shines the queenly love.

Agnes, come nearer, nearer!
And let the *image* be supplanted
By *thyself* so dearer, dearer,
That my paths may be enchanted!
Agnes, how my soul hath panted—
Panteth always to be nearer!

Agnes, my Agnes, prove me!
For all strings of my spirit beat
In harmony of tone, "*I love thee!*"
Evermore I could repeat,
Linkèd with thy life so sweet,
Agnes, my crown, "*I love thee!*"

Agnes, art thou above me?
The magnet of thy perfect mind
Can lift me, if thou love me;
And *doubt* thou lovest were unkind!
Just love me, and I *am* refined!
Agnes, my Agnes, love me!

MY YOUNG WILD RHYME.

One little flower of love I bring,
God touch it with the glow of spring,
And give it tints of more than pearl!
'Tis not a queenly maid I sing,
Nor fancied love of fair young girl,
Nor red-lipped maid of social times,
But her who sings my young wild rhymes.

All of the joys there are for me;
All of the love, the fond, the free;
All of the magic paths o'er-trod,
That stirred all songs of pathos' sea,
And touched with beauty, pureness, God,
Was waked to life in distant times,
When sang she me my young wild rhymes.

How sweet the strong love born at noon;
Or young love hid in heart of June;
Or love of those who wisely wed,
And sad the thought they pass too soon ;
But sweeter far her love, who led
Me from my wayward, boyhood times,
While singing me my young wild rhymes.

BY-AND-BY.

O Nameless, with your holy speaking eye!
O thousand promises of "by-and-by!"
O expectation, born to smile and die!
O "by-and-by," thou *unintended* lie!
Oh! may we not yet realize on high
The promises and all the memory
Of what we *hoped* to have beneath the sky,
At least, above it in *the* by-and-by?

A STAR OF REMINDER.

Fair evening star, and fair Esther!
Crowned both with a curious lustre—
    O wayward two!
Uncheering and drearisome lustre,
    Wearisome hue—
Oh, how did I worship and trust her—
    And evil star, too!

Oh, where such a delicate wooer?
And when were the skies any bluer?
    And when, O star,
Thy gleam any, *seemingly*, truer?
    How near, though far,
You seemed to the delicate wooer
    And me, O star!

A STAR OF REMINDER.

O soul! how could she be kinder
Than, blindly, that night I divined her—
    And star and me—
The night we a star of reminder,
    Sweet star, chose thee?
She gazed, as I stood and entwined her,
    On thee and me.

She said: "Sweet star, in thy glory,
O thou, be the book of our story,
    Pure, mild-eyed star!"
And I said, "Amen!"—But my hurry,
    Too eager, did mar
The book of our love, and a worry
    Crossed, as a spar,
    Our love and our star.

For the vow of my Esther, frail lover!
Sank swift as a meteor rover.—
    Thus swift go down,
Ill star, and the curse of a lover
    Cling to thy crown!
Go out, as a spark, 'neath thy cover
    Of seas, low down—
Since love-looks no more I discover
    In her eyes brown.

FACT vs. FICTION.

BY PETER PRACTICAL.

She was not exquisitely fair ; she was not over sweet ;
She was not super-delicate in the structure of her feet ;
Her locks were not that splendor-cast intended to bewitch ;
And, cutely tangled in their mesh, suspicion saw a "switch"—
Her voice not lute-like, tho' perhaps more sweet than a cicada's,
Her gait not queen-like, tho' as grand as most of other ladies.

She was not tall as tules are, nor built low like a moss ;
She was not slender as the vine, nor broad as oaks across.
Her brow was beauty, not compressed, yet 'twould not waken wonder ;
Her face, that underlay the brow, nor over much nor under.
Her hands were not so large as mine, from which her fingers tapered
That strode through some slow, sad refrain, or down a chorus capered.

Her eyes, like many other eyes, were beautifully blue ;
They were a spirit feast to see ; and yet they were but two

Of many thousand more as full, as deep, as wild, as
    tame ;
Her clear red mellow glow of cheek—all men have
    seen the same.
Her dimples on her cheek and chin had many a duplicate,
And dimples only grow at length to crevices we hate.

In thought, she lived not in the swamp, nor on the
    stormy mountains ;
But on the slopes between the two, drank streams from
    higher fountains.
She had some reason and some wit, some gleams of
    common song,
But all these mingled unobserved with all the common
    throng
Of thoughts that lose themselves at last in those of
    stronger tone
That rush down from the great of earth, who thus are
    greater grown.

She was not wanting in a soul ; hers was conservative,
Not overpowering in its love, nor miserly to give.
Some souls have more divinity, few more of what is
    human ;
In fact hers was conservative, the common soul of
    woman.
Some souls are too divine for me; for my receptive
    measure

Cannot contain them, so the strain gives pain instead
    of pleasure.

The age has reasoned round to this—which seems to
    me a notion—
That love is but a passion now instead of an emotion.
Then I would live below the age (?)—too weak to soar
    above it—
And chloroform that passion love, and wake the truth
    and love it.
I am not lower than the most, nor purer than the mass,
But I would love emotionally my unangelic lass!

She has her brittle thread of life, and separate from
    mine.
We have our common thread of love, fine but not
    superfine.
And should her thread of life be broken, mine might
    be *shaken*, too,
But not be *broken*, as is sung far oftener than true.
My thread of life should be the same, my thread of
    love be finer
By being drawn so to the sky—to regions far *diviner*.

The most of us awake to love in moonlight of our lives,
When those seem angels in the dim, which day reveals
    as wives
Or husbands in their common moods and in their
    common clothes.
And then we talk of "lotteries," and murmur "Ah!
    who knows?"

All should be sleeping in the night and waking in the
   day,
Then fancied angels would not be turned into common
   clay.

The eyes hang heavy in the night ; we see men walk
   as trees,
And shadows seem as living things, and living things
   as these.
And when love holds her wand across the sweet face
   of the moon,
And touches love-strings in the air — intoxicating
   tune !—
Then men seemed turned to demigods, and women
   angels seem,
And we go maddened at the scene, and love is made
   a dream.

Love held her wand across the moon, and chased
   a-down the air
Her fingers on the strings of tune, and *I* went
   maddened there.
I saw my love, with queenly gait, go dancing with
   her shadow ;
The land seemed e'er too beautiful to call an Eldorado.
The trees seemed spanning to the skies, and stars
   seemed blooming on them,
And flowers beneath looked up in love, as though the
   stars had won them.

My love looked down and then looked up, as though
    uncertain whether
The flowers and green mixed in below, or stars and
    blue together,
Were fairer of the spangled two—perplexed, too, with
    her doubt.
The birds went shooting thro', and dropped their
    pearls of song about,
And all the world and all the sky seemed changed
    into the three
Sweet nourishers of living love—song, painting,
    poetry.

But she danced in the midst of all, the angel of the
    scene.
I started through this rhapsody, and ran with bashful
    mien ;
And, as I ran and reached in love, she ever ran ahead;
Yet when I hesitated, aye, I saw it made her sad ;
And when I ran most rapidly, and reached with
    eagerness,
The sweet smile flooding all her face, she could not
    all suppress.

Some go on seeing by the moon, and loving in the
    roses,
Some chase down the delusive form, and rest in sweet
    reposes
Still in the dim light of the night, then waken in the
    dawning

To find the angel they had wed is but a human
    yawning.
Then come the sulky, lonesome hours, in common
    earthly places,
And thinking back to angel-dreams, ahead to human
    faces.

I did not reach my fancy love before the morn was
    on us;
We both stood facing, then, amazed, and wondered
    what had won us.
We kept on wond'ring, till the day eclipsed the
    moonshine folly,
Then turned to common human sense, and turned to
    being jolly.
I love her for the charms she *has*, and not for those
    that *seem*—
This may be tame love, yet this love is better than
    a dream.

LIVE AND LET LIVE.

Strive? to be sure we should strive, till we thrill
   Our being with struggles of muscle and mind.
But, ah! is the world but a cañon-like rill,
   With room but for one and no room to be kind?
Full wide is the river to work and forgive,
Nor tangle our oars as we live and let live.

The diligent hand may wax rich without harm
   To other hands reaching the bounties of life.
But, alas! that so many are cast in a storm
   By those who would gather the wreck of their strife.
We sift all the grain through and leave in the sieve
The chaff for a brother: nor live and let live.

It is nothing humane that we sift the grain thro'
   Then cast to a brother the leavings of chaff.
It is nothing humane that we make a storm strew
   The strength of our foes, as we gather, and quaff
Our glasses of gains, and we smile as they grieve.
He only lives well, who can live and let live.

It is nothing humane if a neighbor should strain
   A weary, thin hand for the gladness of life,
That swords of our avarice strike it and stain
   With blood of defeat the one weaker in strife:
There's a kernel for each in Life's beautiful sieve,
And chaff for the wind, if we live and let live.

There is room on the tide of Life's changeable way
    For all who go rowing to pass and return
And never strike oars, as we sprinkle with spray
    The brothers who pass with the prizes they earn—
With sprays of delight that they win, as we give
Clear way to the weaker, and live and let live.

It is better to wring from inanimate earth,
    By resolute effort, the wealth we desire
Than wring from a brother the wealth he brought forth
    From the tempests of sin, or the furnace of fire.
How many, alas! are refusing to give
Fair way to a foe, and to live and let live.

THE WHITE CRANE.

Tall, white and superb, he is pure as the springs,
   Save wings tipped with black, as if tinged with
      a sin;
And thus, like a saint that has beaten with wings
   A narrow ascent through the sin-snares within
To lands of a better and beautiful birth,
He touched lightly wings on the sins of the earth.

Hear the voices of doves in the trees overhead;
   They soar not aloft in the sky and its coves,
Nor come down below where the maidens so thread
   Their sonnets of love through the leaves of the
      groves;
Nor come down below, nor aspire to the sky,
But coo to the trees and complain till they die.

But the crane, bird of thought in his garments of
      white,
   Speaks strong as a hope in the heart of a youth,
And clear as a knell that is sent in the night,
   With tongue sternly telling a dying man's truth.
His words, strong as sonnets of wisdom, arise;
For seldom he speaketh and hence he is wise.

He walks on the earth till he feels and thus learns
   The wrongs of the lowly; he looks up above

To fields of the good, till his poet-heart burns,
   Then swinging away on his pinions of love,
He circles above to the kiss of a cloud,
Bathed in smiles of the stars that seem speaking aloud.

Let him be as a bard,—as a symbol to show
   How poets may mingle with mortals, whose wrongs
Flood valleys of earth with their rivers of woe,
   Then rising inspired, in the strength of their songs
May lead the strained eyes and the sad hearts within
Up to happier scenes than earth's visions of sin.

He pointeth a moral :—with power in his wings
   And will and a patience to charm, to surprise,
He rises and swings in a pathway of rings
   Till his pinions fan faces of stars as he flies—
The moral is this : That no matter how wise,
He finds he can easier fall than arise.

Majestic, tall, white, as he walketh abroad,
   He says not a word, though he seeth and thinketh ;
But he singeth when circling away unto God !
   So his heaven-heard song gleameth brightly and linketh
Our thoughts to High Heaven. I give you my hand!
Brother, poet and singer ; you will understand !

DEATH OF THE OLD PROFESSOR.

The ebbing hours had worn away
The dusk, and brought the death of day,
Which slowly, peacefully lay breathing
Its last red breath on evening's rim;
O'er the soft grass night dews were wreathing,
When my Professor, old and gray,
Lay dying in the starlit twilight dim.

Students, two-score, with serious eyes
Alight with tears and wreathed with sighs,
Stood round his bed; his dreamy gaze
Saw many hundred men of yore
Look up from chapel seats, ablaze
With glorious golden mem'ry ties—
Bright student faces; now, alas, no more!

The night wore on, and two-score faces,
Love-full, lore-full, took olden places—
Tear-moist and sober; still he smiles,
His soul controlled by fruitful fancy
That, ere he sails to stormless Isles,
He call his roll of many classes;
Thus looks he at the classic files
Of youth, o'er agèd, gold-rimmed glasses,
Marched into place as if by necromancy.—

That roll-book reads, in which were all
In forty years he loved to call!
He then began, with voice so slender,
Death-tremulous, his chapel singing;
And then with tone more childlike, tender,
His roll-call sounds thro' fancied Hall
Of College, dying thus to fancy clinging!

Just as the last name crossed his lips,
Soft, silent as a spirit slips
To isles of joy, his soul crossed over.
Star-crowned, his heart speaks back to me,
In time of snow or days of clover,
While outward sweep my mem'ry-ships,
Whene'er I sit in diamond revery!—

In dreams awake, or dreams asleep,
Whene'er my thoughts lie sad and deep,
From skies above I seem to hear
Him calling rolls from class to class
In mingled pathos and good cheer;
As mem'ry-ships with shoutings sweep
Swift up to Aidenn's stormless pier
I wake from musings sweet to weep,
"How far the portal to '*The Sea of Glass!*'"

TELOUCHKINE.

I.

The spire of great "Saint Peter's and Saint
    Paul's,"
Lost like a needle in the purple skies,
Stood gleaming in the centuries of light
And dwindled, o'er Slavonic, Titan walls
Of grand Saint Petersburg, to fairy size,
A gold-hued world poised on its airy height;
And on this poised unpeopled planet stood
A steadfast *angel*, emblem of the good,
Enshielded blue with heaven's blue amplitude.

II.

Now, by the driving tempests of the skies
And stealing frosts and feathery snowy feet,
It leans to fall, while men, who creep below
Like insects, upward gaze with dust-small eyes
(While aspirations drag the stony street
By leaden fears, and over ever go
The silvery clouds that kiss the angel's face),
And idly speculate, and, skeptic, trace
The gulf impassable of towering space !

III.

But Telouchkine, a tzar uncrownèd, gazed
The airy ocean thro', but not, as they,

With fruitless wondering and helpless thought:
His thoughts in brilliant upward steppings
    blazed—
A vaulting wonder-deed, heroic way
To reach the falling angel! Thus he wrought
A restoration for the seraph King,
Exalted emblem of man's primal spring,
The Eden seraph now with failing wing.

IV.

He clomb the spire!—The shouts of surging
    specks
Came floating up in faint far murmurings
When Telouchkine now by the angel stood!
He scanning downward—upward—little recks
If he be nearer those sweet pearlèd strings
That star the blue at noonday solitude
To one so skyey deep! Brave Telouchkine!
A plain-clad king with crown more superfine
Than Inca's gold and Afric's diamond mine.

V.

For he alone dare win its lofty gleam
Redeeming Russia's angel clothed with gold:—
'*Twas thus with man;* for halting wisdom tried,
And haughty folly, ages, to redeem
The "angel in us" from its ruin old.
'Twas unavailing folly's shallow-eyed
And peering throngs around the Titan wall,
Till Christ came down, and, crownèd King of All,
This "Angel in us" saved from endless fall!

WAYSIDE FLOWERS.

Some feeble wayside flowers, in sterile ground,
That bloomed in love to cast their sweetness round
To gladden hearts, who shifted by the sweet
And tender blossoms nodding at their feet,
Nor thought to thank the slender angel flowers
That cheered them thro' their weary journey-hours!

www.ingramcontent.com/pod-product-compliance
Lightning Source LLC
Chambersburg PA
CBHW020128170426
43199CB00009B/683